BIOGRAPHIC
PRINCE

BIOGRAPHIC
PRINCE

LIZ FLAVELL

ILLUSTRATED BY
MATT CARR

AMMONITE
PRESS

www.ammonitepress.com

Text © Liz Flavell, 2020
Copyright in the Work © GMC Publications Ltd, 2020

ISBN 978 1 78145 407 7

Publisher: Jason Hook
Concept Design: Matt Carr
Design & Illustration: Matt Carr & Robin Shields
Editor: Laura Paton

Colour reproduction by GMC Reprograph
Printed and bound in Turkey

CONTENTS

ICONOGRAPHIC

WHEN WE CAN RECOGNIZE A MUSICIAN BY
A SET OF ICONS, WE CAN ALSO RECOGNIZE
HOW COMPLETELY THAT ARTIST AND
THEIR MUSIC HAVE ENTERED OUR
CULTURE AND OUR CONSCIOUSNESS.

INTRODUCTION

Pure talent is rare. Rarer still is pure talent combined with vision, creativity, determination and an unfailing work ethic. Prince Rogers Nelson was one of the few artists to embody all these attributes. An undisputed musical genius, he became synonymous with genre-bending approaches, imaginative compositions and highly sexualized lyrics, attracting millions of devoted fans worldwide and securing his place in pop music's hall of fame.

In that interview with Oprah, Prince did offer a few clues to the origins of his flamboyant and workaholic identity. Growing up in Minneapolis, he had been bullied on account of his small stature, and had responded by developing an alternative persona. Having seen his father performing in his jazz trio, Prince saw where his own path lay, and immersed himself in music and fantasy. Playing piano became an escape both from bullying and an unsettled family life, just as in later life endless hours in the studio became the panacea for everything.

Prince's career took off in 1982 with the release of his double album *1999* and first hit single 'Little Red Corvette'. In 1984, the purple phenomenon went global with the film, soundtrack and hit single that all shared the same name, 'Purple Rain'. Fans and critics describe the song as his masterpiece, but over the next 30 years he went on to unleash a torrent of hits traversing the genres of pop, funk, soul, rock, rap and jazz.

The 1980s was the age of the music video and Prince had the self-assurance, showmanship and sexually charged energy required of an MTV star. The ultimate performer, he stunned audiences with outrageous costumes and hairstyles, gymnastic dance moves and exceptional guitar licks. Yet, off stage and off screen, Prince remained something of an enigma, and guarded his privacy closely. Revelatory interviews were rare. Even when Oprah Winfrey visited him at Paisley Park in 1996, he concealed the tragic and recent death of his newborn son, Amiir, telling Oprah that things were "all good".

Prince's career kicked off in the clubs of Minneapolis where he carved out a unique synth-pop sound and an equally original look, sometimes sporting little more than black underpants and an artful necktie. Onstage and in the studio he was experimental, explicit and exciting. On his first album *For You*, released in 1978, Prince was credited with playing 27 instruments. Creating music dominated his entire existence and he skipped meals, sleep and normal life to build his repertoire and his career.

Music poured out of Prince, and it was accompanied by a fierce desire to determine his own way in the music business and release his songs as and when he wanted, not when his label dictated. In 1992, disputes with Warner Bros escalated and he daubed 'SLAVE' on his face during live performances. The following year he changed his name to a symbol and was famously referred to as 'the Artist Formerly Known as Prince'.

Ties with Warner Bros were finally severed in 2000 and Prince took back his name. He became a Jehovah's Witness, but his new-found spirituality did not diminish his musical output. Standout performances included the Grammys with Beyoncé in 2004, the Rock & Roll Hall of Fame tribute to George Harrison the same year and the Super Bowl Halftime show in 2007 – 'Sexy MF' no longer made the playlist but Prince was at the top of his game.

"WHEN PRINCE WAS IN THE STUDIO, IT LOOKED LIKE HE WAS MAKING A SALAD. HE WAS THROWING TAPE AROUND LIKE A CHEF."

—Chuck D, Public Enemy, 2019

In that interview in 1996 when Oprah asked how many songs he had left in him, Prince revealed: "One a day...until I die." He remained remarkably prolific, and after his untimely death on 21 April 2016 it was discovered that the Vault at Paisley Park contained enough unreleased material to fill a new album every year for the next century.

Prince's existence at Paisley Park combined the two aspects of his personality. At times he lived a seemingly normal life, riding his bicycle into Minneapolis, knocking on doors to proclaim his faith and playing table tennis or basketball (albeit in platform heels!). But he also lived a life of excess, whether in the parties he threw, the thousands of shoes he wore, the pills he popped or the mass of recordings he made.

In *Biographic: Prince*, we use infographics to try to capture the nature of this excess and to show how, in its most artistic form, it unleashed a purple patch of creativity in writing, producing, singing, playing and performing that elevated Prince to the highest ranks of rock royalty.

"REALLY, I'M NORMAL. A LITTLE HIGHLY STRUNG, MAYBE. BUT NORMAL. BUT SO MUCH HAS BEEN WRITTEN ABOUT ME AND PEOPLE NEVER KNOW WHAT'S RIGHT AND WHAT'S WRONG. I'D RATHER LET THEM STAY CONFUSED."

—Prince, 2004

PRINCE ROGERS NELSON

01
LIFE

"MUSIC IS EVERYTHING TO ME. I LOVE MAKING MUSIC. I AM MAKING MUSIC. MUSIC IS SPIRIT, IT'S THERAPY. IT MAKES ME FEEL A CERTAIN WAY, AND IF PLAYED WITH CONVICTION AND SOUL, THE SAME THING OCCURS IN OTHER PEOPLE."

—Prince, interview with Mick Brown,
Daily Telegraph, 2004

MINNESOTA

UNITED STATES
OF AMERICA

MINNESOTA ROYALTY

Lizzo collaborated with Prince on his 2014 album *Plectrumelectrum.* Born in Detroit in 1988, she had been part of the rap scene in Minneapolis since moving there in 2011.

Bob Dylan was born in Duluth, Minnesota, in 1941. Dylan enrolled at the University of Minnesota in 1959 and started playing the folk clubs around the city.

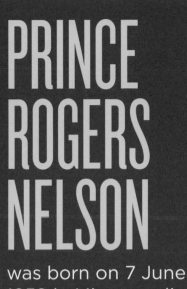

PRINCE ROGERS NELSON

was born on 7 June 1958 in Minneapolis, Minnesota, USA

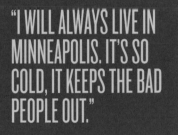

"I WILL ALWAYS LIVE IN MINNEAPOLIS. IT'S SO COLD, IT KEEPS THE BAD PEOPLE OUT."

—Prince, quoted in the *Daily Mail*, 2016

Prince was born in Mount Sinai Hospital in the city of Minneapolis. He was given his regal name by his pianist father John L. Nelson, who had always dreamed of fame for himself and hoped his son might realize that dream. John was a plastic moulder in an electronics factory by day and played with a jazz trio at night. Prince's mother, Mattie Della, was a jazz singer.

Prince's parents separated when he was seven but his hometown of Minneapolis remained a constant throughout his life. It was where he developed the sound that transformed him into a musical legend. It was also the only place he felt safe enough to cycle on his own, something he did pretty much to his dying day. The last photos taken of Prince show him on his bicycle as he makes his way home from a local drugstore the night before he died.

LIFE

THE MUSIC WORLD IN 1958

When Prince was born in 1958, the Second World War was becoming a distant memory. In that year, the peace symbol was invented, and life was beginning to swing again. Rock 'n' roll was king, and the king of rock 'n' roll was Elvis Presley. The Sixties, and The Beatles, were on the horizon. NASA was founded and the microchip was invented; the world's first satellite, Soviet Union's Sputnik I, had orbited Earth in October 1957, and the Space Age was dawning. It was the start of a modern revolutionary world fit for a prince, and a time when anything really did feel possible.

OCTOBER

James Brown's 'Try Me' is released. It will top the R&B chart in February 1959.

MARCH

Billie Holiday is given a year's probation in Philadelphia for possession of narcotics.

ON THE JUKEBOX

'Sweet Little Sixteen' – Chuck Berry
'At the Hop' – Danny and The Juniors
'Get a Job' – The Silhouettes
'Tequila' – The Champs
'Twilight Time' – The Platters
'Yakety Yak' – The Coasters
'Splish Splash' – Bobby Darin

MAY

Jerry Lee Lewis's UK tour ends when the press uncovers his marriage to 13-year-old second cousin Myra Gale Brown.

JULY

The Beatles (still named The Quarrymen) have their first recording session.

AUGUST

Cliff Richard's 'Move It' charts to become the first rock 'n' roll hit recorded outside the USA.

MARCH

Elvis enters the US Army and is posted to Germany.

TOP SELLER IN UK

First song to debut at No. 1 in UK chart

ELVIS PRESLEY • JAILHOUSE ROCK

3 WEEKS AT NO. 1

ALSO BORN IN 1958

Kate Bush (above), 30 July
Bruce Dickinson, 7 August
Madonna, 16 August
Michael Jackson, 29 August
Andrea Bocelli, 22 September
Joan Jett, 22 September
Nikki Sixx, 11 December

TOP SELLER IN USA

Domenico Modugno, 'Volare (Nel blu dipinto di blu)'

Five weeks at No. 1 in Billboard charts

Record of the Year at the 1st Annual Grammy Awards

HALF SISTER
Lorna L. Nelson
(1943–2006)

FATHER'S
FIRST WIFE
Vivian Nelson
(1920–73)

FATHER
John Lewis Nelson
(1916–2001)

HALF SISTER
Norrine Nelson
(b. 1947)

HALF BROTHER
John R. Nelson
(b. 1948)

HALF SISTER
Sharon L. Nelson
(b. 1942)

Prince
Rogers Nelson
(1958–2016)

HALF BROTHER
Duane Nelson
(1958–2011)

FIRST WIFE
Mayte Janell
Garcia
(b. 1973)

SECOND
WIFE
Manuela
Testolini
(b. 1976)

Married
to Prince
1996–2000

SON
Amiir Gregory
Nelson
(b. & d. 1996)

Born with Pfeiffer
syndrome type 2, Amiir
lived for six days. Amiir is
Arabic for 'Prince'.

Married
to Prince
2001–6

PRINCE

18

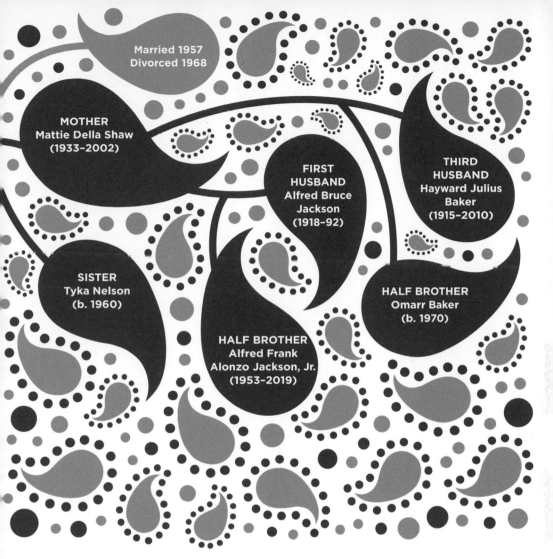

Married 1957
Divorced 1968

MOTHER
Mattie Della Shaw
(1933–2002)

FIRST HUSBAND
Alfred Bruce Jackson
(1918–92)

THIRD HUSBAND
Hayward Julius Baker
(1915–2010)

SISTER
Tyka Nelson
(b. 1960)

HALF BROTHER
Omarr Baker
(b. 1970)

HALF BROTHER
Alfred Frank Alonzo Jackson, Jr.
(1953–2019)

THE ROYAL FAMILY

Prince's father John L. Nelson was playing with his jazz band, the Prince Rogers Trio, when he hooked up with Prince's mother Mattie. She was around sixteen years younger than John, but they made a stylish couple. As a child, Prince loved watching his sharply dressed parents get ready for their nights out – Mattie in beautifully coordinated outfits and John in immaculate suits with sparkling cufflinks. But however they dressed things up, the marriage was breaking down. Prince's parents separated when he was seven and divorced when he was ten. He spent a few years with his mother before moving to his father's, where he found solace composing tunes on the upright piano.

LITTLE PRINCE

Prince's earliest memories were of his mother's loving eyes, the sound of his father playing the piano and *Superman* on the television. He attended John Hay Elementary School, where he countered being teased for his small stature by being "flashy and noisy", traits that would endure. He was mesmerized when he first saw his father onstage, and he started buying records, transcribing the lyrics and teaching himself to play the music. Minneapolis radio stations such as KQRS played tunes by black and white artists that would influence Prince. He was a Joni Mitchell fan, but James Brown was his main man.

Aged seven, Prince teaches himself to play the piano, and writes his first song, 'Funk Machine'.

Prince moves in with his aunt, Olivia. She doesn't have a piano, so his father buys him his first guitar.

1965 1966 1967 1968 1969 1970 1971 1972

John and Mattie divorce and Prince lives mostly with his mother.

Prince attends Bryant Junior High where he enjoys sport, particularly basketball. When his mother meets a new man, Prince moves in with his father but is kicked out after being caught in bed with a girl.

Aged 15, Prince joins his first band, Grand Central, and plays gigs after school. By now he's regularly crashing at band member Andre Anderson's house and is taking a Business of Music course.

Prince's first record deal with Warner Bros was a three-album deal for a cool **$1,000,000**

Prince plays guitar for local band 94 East and co-writes 'Just Another Sucker'.

The first demos Prince records at Sound 80 studios in Minneapolis secure him a contract with Warner Bros. Prince leaves Minneapolis for California where he records his first album at Record Plant studios in Sausalito.

After forming his band The Revolution, Prince releases his self-titled second album. The single 'I Wanna Be Your Lover' goes platinum and becomes his first Top 40 hit.

1973 1974 1975 1976 1977 1978 1979 1980

Finding Central High School "a drag", Prince spends his time at Chris Moon's studio in Minneapolis, learning how to use a mixing desk to blend synth-pop, new wave and funk into a new sound.

Prince releases debut album *For You*, which reaches 163 in the charts. He buys his first house and creates his first studio in the basement.

Prince pours his heart, soul and sexuality into his third album *Dirty Mind*, saying: "If I could put my bloodstream on vinyl, then this is what it would be." Recorded in his home basement studio, the album would be certified gold.

FORMERLY KNOWN AS...

In 1991, Warner Bros Records filed a trademark with the United States Patent and Trademark Office for Prince in the categories of printed materials, clothing, electronic commerce and entertainment services. The trademark allowed them to profit both from Prince's work and his name. Less than two years later, while discussing his new album with the label, Prince argued that he should retain artistic and financial control, something they refused. The disagreement led to a lawsuit between the two parties, and Prince later appeared in public with the word 'SLAVE' written on his cheek. In his attempts to escape his contract, Prince changed his name to the unpronounceable 'Love Symbol', and in the press he was referred to as 'the Artist Formerly Known as Prince'. When this ruse was unsuccessful, Prince began to release albums in quick succession as a means of liberating himself from his contractual obligations to Warner Bros. Three years later, with his contract fulfilled, Prince returned as... Prince.

THE 'LOVE SYMBOL' WAS BORN FROM THE MERGING OF THE MALE AND FEMALE SYMBOLS.

FEMALE

MALE

"RECORD CONTRACTS ARE JUST LIKE – I'M GONNA SAY THE WORD – SLAVERY. I WOULD TELL ANY YOUNG ARTIST... DON'T SIGN."

—Prince, 2015

PRINCE'S PSEUDONYMS / NICKNAMES

HELLO my name is
ALEXANDER NEVERMIND

HELLO my name is
CAMILLE

HELLO my name is
CHRISTOPHER

HELLO my name is
CHRISTOPHER TRACY

HELLO my name is
ERIC BRAZIL

HELLO my name is
JAMIE STARR

HELLO my name is
JOEY COCO

HELLO my name is
LOVE SYMBOL

HELLO my name is
MADHOUSE

HELLO my name is
PAISLEY PARK

HELLO my name is
PETER BRAVESTRONG

HELLO my name is
TAFKAP

HELLO my name is
THE STARR COMPANY

HELLO my name is
TORA TORA

HELLO my name is
THE HIGH PRIEST OF POP

HELLO my name is
HIS ROYAL BADNESS

HELLO my name is
THE PRINCE OF FUNK

HELLO my name is
THE PURPLE ONE

ICONIC LOOKS

1984
PURPLE RAIN TOUR

As worn in the movie, Prince's touring outfit included a purple sequinned jacket, white ruffled shirt and purple velvet trousers.

1988
LOVESEXY TOUR

This simple black shirt and white tailored trousers combination could have looked boring if not for the addition of contrasting polka dots.

1994
VH1 AWARDS

Prince wowed with a deep-cut, V-neck white shirt and trousers. Accessories included sunglasses, oversized gold chain and a cane.

The look was almost as important to Prince as the music, and throughout his career he mixed different fashion styles and played around with gender. Every day was an opportunity to dress up at Paisley Park, and he wore his trademark heels even when playing basketball. It took a ten-strong team of tailors to make the outfits for Prince and his band, all to his exact specifications, resulting in a series of iconic looks.

2004
GRAMMY AWARDS

Prince performed in a double-breasted tailored suit with shoulder pads, all in Prince purple, and a gold shirt, tie and pocket square.

2010
WELCOME 2 AMERICA TOUR

This dazzling gold roll-neck jumpsuit was covered from head to toe with sequins. The look was finished off with matching gilded heels.

2015
AMA AWARDS

Prince donned a gold snakeskin vest on top of a yellow flared shirt, accessorized with the now iconic third-eye sunglasses.

PURPLE PATCH

1981

Prince's raunchy wardrobe and music prove too much for the audience when he opens for The Rolling Stones in LA, and he is booed off stage.

1982

The 'Little Red Corvette' video plays on MTV as Prince and Michael Jackson become the first black artists to appear on the channel.

1996

'The Artist Formerly Known as Prince' marries Mayte Janelle Garcia, a 22-year-old dancer who has been part of his troupe since she was a teenager.

Their six-day-old child, Amiir Gregory Nelson, dies.

Prince releases *Chaos and Disorder*, his last album for Warner Bros.

1993

Feuding with Warner Bros, on his 35th birthday Prince changes his name to the 'Love Symbol' and appears live with 'SLAVE' written on his face.

1990

Forms the New Power Generation.

1999

Signs to Arista Records.

2000

Divorces Mayte. When his publishing deal with Warner Bros expires, Prince goes by his own name again.

2016

Final concert of the worldwide Piano & A Microphone Tour takes place at the Fox Theatre in Atlanta; last song is 'Purple Rain'. At 10.07am on 21 April, Prince is pronounced dead at Paisley Park.

2015

Prince releases his final album, *HITnRUN Phase Two*.

2014

Signs with Warner Bros again. Performs intimate gigs including one at the London home of young singer Lianne La Havas.

1984

Forms his band The Revolution, comprising Lisa Coleman, Matt 'Doctor' Fink, Bobby Z, Brown Mark, Dez Dickerson and, later that year, Wendy Melvoin.

1985

Wins an Oscar for Best Original Score for *Purple Rain.* Later in the year, he gives his first interview in three years with *Rolling Stone* magazine.

1989

Writes the score for Tim Burton's *Batman* movie. The LP later tops the charts.

1987

Disbands The Revolution.

1986

No. 1 in the US with 'Kiss'; 'Manic Monday' by The Bangles (which he also wrote) is at No. 2. Releases his second film, *Under a Cherry Moon.*

Construction of Prince's recording studio and future home, Paisley Park, commences in Minneapolis.

2001

Becomes a Jehovah's Witness, marries Manuela Testolini and launches the NPG Music Club, his own music subscription service.

2004

Inducted into the Rock and Roll Hall of Fame. *Rolling Stone* magazine claims Prince is the highest-earning musician on the planet.

2006

Divorces Manuela. The NPG Music Club is shut down. Prince opens a nightclub in Las Vegas called 3121 and performs there every weekend until April 2007.

2011

Purple Rain is inducted into the Grammy Hall of Fame.

2007

Gives his legendary performance at the Super Bowl XLI Halftime Show. Gives away free copies of the album *Planet Earth* to promote 21 shows at London's O2 Arena (below).

MEDICAL NOTES

In the months leading up to Prince's death, he had lost weight and cancelled a number of gigs on the Piano & A Microphone Tour because of 'flu'. Some newspapers suggested that the star had AIDS. On the evening of 15 April 2016, after a gig in Atlanta, Prince's private jet made an emergency landing in Moline, Illinois. Prince was rushed to hospital and given a shot of Narcan, the drug administered for opioid overdoses. Prince was famed for his clean living, so the news was a surprise to many. His dependency on painkilling drugs only became apparent after his death.

154

The number of hours straight that Prince worked before he died

ARTHRITIC HIPS

Prince refused a double hip operation, possibly because of religious beliefs. He relied on the painkiller Percocet, until 2010 when he finally underwent surgery at Mayo Clinic, Rochester, Minnesota.

When Prince was hospitalized on 15 April, doctors recommended he stay 24 hours but he stayed only

3 HOURS

SHOE SIZE

American women's size

5.5/6

Prince weighed only
112lb (50.8kg)
at the time of his death.

EPILEPSY

Diagnosed at birth, he suffered seizures throughout his childhood.

27in. (68cm)
WAIST

5ft 3in. (160cm)

WALKING CANE

Prince carried a cane in his late 40s (people thought it was part of the act, but he possibly needed it).

ANKLE AND KNEE PAIN

As early as the Purple Rain Tour of 1984–5, Prince was in constant pain from jumping off speakers in high heels.

FENTANYL FATALITIES

Prince was found slumped in the elevator at Paisley Park on the morning of 21 April 2016. Six weeks later, the results of an autopsy revealed that he had died from an accidental overdose of fentanyl. The concentration of the drug in his system was well above that found in other fentanyl victims, suggesting that Prince had been taking the drug over a long period of time.

FENTANYL LEVELS

in the blood that can be fatal:

DEADLY LEVELS

MICROGRAMS PER LITRE

Duration of fentanyl's analgesic effect:

30 – 90

MINUTES

3 – 58

67.8

Fentanyl level in Prince's blood

FENTANYL STREET NAMES

- FRIEND
- APACHE
- GOOD FELLA
- JACKPOT
- TANGO & CASH
- MURDER 8
- CHINA GIRL
- CHINA WHITE
- DANCE FEVER

STRENGTH

30 – 50 times more potent than heroin

50 – 100 times more potent than morphine

TOM PETTY

Died: 2 October 2017
Age: 66
Drugs in system:
fentanyl, celexa
oxycodone, xanax
and restoril

Fentanyl can be taken as a powder, intravenously or as a lollipop.

I GRAM

of pure fentanyl
can be cut to make

7,000

street doses.

80% The increase of fatal overdoses from fentanyl in the US between 2013 and 2014

PURPLE PAIN

The day Prince died, his records were played back to back on radio stations and at the First Avenue nightclub in Minneapolis, where he had launched his career in the 1970s. Buildings, bridges, towers and signs around the world were illuminated in purple. Magazines and newspapers paid homage with purple mastheads. Now the prince was dead, his significance as an artist seemed suddenly to strike home, and everything was covered in purple rain.

21 APRIL 2016

Within hours of Prince's death, Google paid homage on its homepage with purple rain falling on its purple Google logo.

Snapchat honoured Prince with a purple rain filter for the day.

Esther Osayande's 'Purple Raindrop' was erected in Farview Park, Minneapolis, in 2018.

On 2 May 2016, *The New Yorker* magazine paid tribute with its stunning Bob Staake front cover, 'Purple Rain'.

In Paris, the Eiffel Tower (1,063ft high) put on a shimmering purple display.

PRINCE ROGERS NELSON

02
WORLD

"HE'D GET ME TO PLAY A CHARACTER IN THE 'MOVIE' OF THE SONG. HE WAS THE SCREENWRITER, THE ACTOR AND THE PRODUCER. THAT'S HOW

HE LOOKED AT ALL OF HIS PROJECTS. THAT'S HOW HE LOOKS AT HIS CAREER. HIS WHOLE LIFE IS A MOVIE. HE INVENTED HIMSELF."

—Eric Leeds, saxophone and flute
for Prince 1985–2004

HOME IS WHERE THE HEART IS

In the 1970s, Prince created the 'Minneapolis sound' and with the success of the *Purple Rain* album and movie put his hometown on the map. In his lifetime, he acquired homes in Los Angeles, Toronto and Marbella in Spain but he always returned to the city of his birth. "I like Hollywood," he said, "I just like Minneapolis a little better."

1 SOUND 80

222 SOUTH 9TH ST

Guinness World Records calls it 'the oldest multi-track digital recording studio in the world'. Prince recorded demos here for his 1978 debut album *For You*. It's also where Bob Dylan recorded some of *Blood on the Tracks*.

2 CAPRI THEATRE

2027 WEST BROADWAY AVE

Prince played debut gigs as a solo artist on 5 and 6 January 1979. Tickets cost

$4

3 FIRST AVENUE & 7TH STREET ENTRY

701 1ST AVE NORTH

Two music venues in the same building. First Avenue was a location for Prince's 1984 film *Purple Rain*; 531 stars now adorn the exterior to commemorate the famous artists who have played here, including Prince, Bob Dylan and Nirvana.

5 PARK AVE UNITED METHODIST CHURCH

3400 PARK AVE SOUTH

Prince married Mayte Garcia here on 14 February 1996.

4 GLAM SLAM

110 NORTH 5TH ST

Glamorous nightclub Prince opened in 1989, named after his song from the album *Lovesexy*. Prince owned the club for eight years.

Glam Slam has a huge neon entrance.

6 BUNKERS BAR AND GRILL

761 WASHINGTON AVE NORTH

Prince regularly dropped in to the music bar to jam.

7 DAKOTA JAZZ CLUB

1010 NICOLLET MALL

Common haunt for Prince and venue for 'surprise' gigs.

PAISLEY PARK: 22 MILES (35KM)
from central Minneapolis

"I LIVE IN A SMALL TOWN, AND I ALWAYS WILL. I CAN WALK AROUND AND BE ME. THAT'S ALL I WANT TO BE, THAT'S ALL I EVER TRIED TO BE."

—Prince, MTV, 1995

ELECTRIC FETUS

2000 4TH AVE SOUTH

One of Prince's favourite record stores, he made his final visit five days before he died and bought six CDs:

Chamber Brothers: *The Time Has Come*

Joni Mitchell: *Hejira*

Swan Silvertones: *Inspirational Gospel Classics*

Missing Persons: *The Best of Missing Persons*

Santana: *Santana IV*

Stevie Wonder: *Talking Book*

THE HOUSE FROM PURPLE RAIN

3420 SNELLING AVE

The three-bedroom house where 'The Kid', played by Prince, lived in the movie. Prince paid $110,000 for the house in 2015.

STEVIE WONDER
TALKING BOOK

CAN I GET A WITNESS?

Having flaunted his sexual nature and played with androgynous looks in his early career, it surprised many when Prince came out in 2001... as a Jehovah's Witness. Prince was no stranger to the Christian faith: he had always believed in God and had been raised as a Seventh-day Adventist. He was introduced to his new faith by Larry Graham, singer and bass player of Sly and the Family Stone. Prince embraced the core beliefs of the Jehovah's Witnesses and attended the local Kingdom Hall. He even made the house calls expected of each Witness, which must have been a surprise to some residents. Sexually explicit songs were dropped from his live sets and a swear box – 'the cuss bucket' – was installed at Paisley Park. The 2001 album *The Rainbow Children* explored themes of religion, spirituality, sex and racism.

1870s
The religion is founded in the USA

1879
***Zion's Watch Tower* magazine is founded**

8.6 MILLION
Approximate number of practising Witnesses

300,000
Estimated number of new members each year

144,000
The number of people who will go to heaven when 'the end' comes

740
The estimated number of house calls it takes to make a convert

10
The hours per month a Witness should commit to house-to-house calling

5
The times a week practising Witnesses are expected to attend sacred meetings

FAMOUS WITNESSES

Prince

Venus and
Serena Williams

Hank Williams

The Notorious B.I.G.

Patti Smith · · · · · · · · · ·

Michael Jackson

In Nazi concentration
camps, Jehovah's
Witness prisoners
were Identified
by a purple
triangle.

1914

The year they
believe the
'End Times'
began

2001

Prince becomes
a Jehovah's
Witness

ISAIAH 43:10
The Bible passage from which
the Jehovah's Witnesses get
their name.

MATTHEW 28:19
The Bible passage that
proposes door-to-door
evangelism.

LUKE 10:1
Jesus sends the 72 followers
out in pairs, which is why
Witnesses always work
in pairs.

BELIEFS

God the Father is called 'Jehovah'
and he created everything.

Jesus Christ is the firstborn son of
God. He was created by God and,
though he is mighty, he is inferior
to God.

The Holy Spirit is an active force
used by God to accomplish his will.

Jesus died on a stake rather than a
cross, so Witnesses do not use the
cross as a symbol.

Humans do not have an immortal
soul. When a person dies, their
existence ceases. However, death is
not the end of everything; a person
can be resurrected.

DANCING KINGS

Prince took ballet training at Minnesota Dance Theatre as a teen, but it wasn't until the release of the video for 'Little Red Corvette' (1983) that the splits, the spins and the funky steps came together to such breathtaking effect. By 1986, in the video for 'Kiss', Prince was showcasing not only his finely toned abs but also his effortless moves in one of the most sexually charged of all dance performances. Choreography remained a scintillating part of Prince's act, evolving with each new musical direction. Even in his 50s, in considerable pain, he was still performing those epic splits. Prince often claimed James Brown was his inspiration but his moves have also been compared with Mick Jagger's and his style attributed to Bob Fosse. So, how did his shoes and his moves measure up in the world of modern dance?

SHOE SIZE: 9 US

BOB FOSSE (1927–87)

Dancer, theatre and film director, choreographer

Unique, sexy jazz style that influenced Prince's moves

HEIGHT: 5ft 8in. (173cm)

TOP SPOT: Choreography for 'The Rich Man's Frug' in the movie *Sweet Charity*

SIGNATURE SHOES: Black suede lace-up dance shoes

FRED ASTAIRE (1899–1987)

Dancer, singer, actor, choreographer

Possibly the most influential dancer in musical film

HEIGHT: 5ft 9in. (175cm)

TOP SPOT: Tap routine in the movie *Top Hat*

SIGNATURE SHOES: Brown two-tone leather spectators

SHOE SIZE: 8.5 US

PRINCE (1958–2016)

Singer, multi-instrumentalist, dancer, producer

All-round entertainer who juggled sensational guitar riffs with funky moves

HEIGHT: 5ft 3in. (160cm)

TOP SPOT: Slinky slides, splits and sultry stares in video for 'Kiss'

SIGNATURE SHOES: Black suede Andre No. 1 heels with 'Love Symbol' zip

SHOE SIZE: 5.5/6 US

GENE KELLY (1912–96)

Dancer, film actor, choreographer, singer, film director

Charismatic movie star with athletic, balletic style

HEIGHT: 5ft 7in. (171cm)

TOP SPOT: 'Singin' in the Rain', possibly the most iconic scene in a musical film

SIGNATURE SHOES: Brown penny loafers

SHOE SIZE: 8.5 US

MICHAEL JACKSON (1958–2009)

Singer, dancer, 'moonwalker'

Prince's rival in music and dance, whom Fred Astaire called 'extraordinary'

HEIGHT: 5ft 9in. (175cm)

TOP SPOT: Moonwalk in live footage of 'Billie Jean'

SIGNATURE SHOES: Florsheim Imperial black leather loafers, or 'magic shoes'

SHOE SIZE: 9.5 US

LET'S GO SPORT CRAZY!

MINNESOTA

Prince supported local football team Minnesota Vikings, who play in his beloved purple and gold. After watching them win a playoff against the Dallas Cowboys in 2010, he went straight to the studio to record 'Purple and Gold' as a rousing team song.

SPORTING ARTISTS

JACK JOHNSON was a pro surfer.

BRITNEY SPEARS played point guard for her high school basketball team.

BRUCE DICKINSON once ranked seventh at fencing in Britain.

JULIO IGLESIAS played in goal for Real Madrid.

BOB MARLEY was a football fanatic who played daily at home and on tour.

SUPER BOWL XLI
**Dolphin Stadium, near Miami
4 February 2007**

INDIANAPOLIS COLTS V CHICAGO BEARS

At Super Bowl XLI, Prince gave one of the great half-time shows, culminating in an extraordinary and emotional performance of 'Purple Rain' played on a purple 'Love Symbol' stage, with a purple 'Love Symbol' guitar, in a stadium illuminated in purple, beneath a divinely timed torrential downpour. Asked before the show if he wanted to cancel the performance due to the weather, he had replied: "Can you make it rain harder?"

Some psychologists suggest there is a connection between musical genius and athletic prowess, and Prince seemed to bear this out. At Bryant Junior High and Central High he played point guard for the basketball team, and he had a basketball court installed at Paisley Park next to the studio. A table-tennis table is also still there, testament to the Purple One's love of sport and competition in many different forms.

"I REALLY BELIEVE [BASKETBALL] WAS HIS FIRST LOVE. HE WAS VERY SMALL. BUT HE WAS QUICK. HE COULD HANDLE THE BALL AND HE COULD PENETRATE AND HE COULD DISH."

—Al Nuness, basketball coach, Minneapolis Central High School

BRYANT
3

Prince wore the No. 3 shirt at Bryant Junior High School.

Prince was a fan of his hometown basketball teams: the NBA's Minnesota Timberwolves and the WNBA's Minnesota Lynx. He was in the crowd in 2015 when the Lynx won the WNBA championship, and invited the team back to Paisley Park for a three-hour long concert and party.

Watch the video of Prince's 2004 track 'The Daisy Chain' and at 5 minutes 37 seconds you'll be rewarded with the only known footage of Prince playing basketball at Paisley Park.

PRINCE V JACKO

Prince was a talented table-tennis player, and the story goes that Michael Jackson was not thrilled when heavily defeated on the table at Paisley Park in 2004.

Compilation albums were big news in the 1980s, as were blockbuster movies, epic videos, big hair, extreme make-up and enormous shoulder pads. Excess was everywhere, and nowhere more so than in the music industry. Prince's look, sound, production and dance moves were decade defining, and if his record company had let him off the leash then he'd have been on every compilation album going. Madonna, Michael Jackson and Billy Joel were other big players in the decade that knew how to do it large.

BESTSELLERS

UK	US
⬤ **Single**	◯ **Single**
⬤ **Album**	◯ **Album**

1980

'Don't Stand So Close To Me' (The Police)

Super Trouper (Abba)

'Call Me' (Blondie)

The Wall (Pink Floyd)

1981

'Tainted Love' (Soft Cell)

Kings of the Wild Frontier (Adam and The Ants)

'Bette Davis Eyes' (Kim Carnes)

Hi Infidelity (REO Speedwagon)

NOW THAT'S WHAT

Prince spent

378 WEEKS

on the US Billboard Chart in the 1980s – longer than any other artist.

1982

'Come On Eileen' (Dexys Midnight Runners)

Love Songs (Barbra Streisand)

'Physical' (Olivia Newton-John)

Asia (Asia)

1983

'Karma Chameleon' (Culture Club)

Thriller (Michael Jackson)

'Every Breath You Take' (The Police)

Thriller (Michael Jackson)

1989

'Ride on Time' (Black Box)

Ten Good Reasons (Jason Donovan)

'Look Away' (Chicago)

Don't Be Cruel (Bobby Brown)

 1988

'Mistletoe and Wine' (Cliff Richard)

Kylie (Kylie Minogue)

'Faith' (George Michael)

Faith (George Michael)

WE CALLED MUSIC

1987

'Never Gonna Give You Up' (Rick Astley)

Bad (Michael Jackson)

'Walk Like an Egyptian' (The Bangles)

Slippery When Wet (Bon Jovi)

Rolling Stone magazine named Prince and The Revolution's 1984 album *Purple Rain* the second best album of the decade (behind *London Calling* by The Clash).

1986

'Don't Leave Me This Way' (The Communards)

True Blue (Madonna)

'That's What Friends Are For' (Dionne Warwick)

Whitney Houston (Whitney Houston)

 1984

'Do They Know It's Christmas?' (Band Aid)

Can't Slow Down (Lionel Richie)

'When Doves Cry' (Prince and The Revolution)

Thriller (Michael Jackson)

1985

'The Power of Love' (Jennifer Rush)

Brothers in Arms (Dire Straits)

'Careless Whisper' (George Michael)

Born in the USA (Bruce Springsteen)

WHO COMPARES 2 U?

6'6"

6'

5'6"

5'

4'6"

4'

3'6"

3'

2'6"

2'

1'6"

1'

0

PRINCE

JAMES BROWN

5'3"
(160cm)

5'6"
(168cm)

Prince was noted for his small stature. Standing at about 5ft 3in., he is possibly the smallest male megastar of all time. To emphasize this, he often surrounded himself with female dancers and band members who towered over him, such as Wendy and Lisa from Prince and The Revolution. He famously wore high heels to give him height, and this ultimately contributed to his death. Years of performing in platform heels caused hip problems in later life, which in turn led to a dependency on painkillers.

MICHAEL JACKSON

STEVIE WONDER

MARVIN GAYE

5'9"
(175cm)

6'1"
(185cm)

6'1"
(185cm)

23 POSITIONS

Prince was a naughty boy until he mounted the Watchtower and became a Jehovah's Witness. Before that, his lyrics and his provocative act knew few bounds, and it was Prince who provoked the introduction of the Parental Advisory sticker. One mother was so outraged at his lyrics for 'Darling Nikki' (for the record, the bit about masturbation and magazines) that she petitioned for warning stickers to be slapped on the cover of records or CDs with profane or sexually explicit lyrics. It's hard to find an early Prince album without a song that wasn't worthy of a sticker: 'Head' (1980), 'Jack U Off' (1981), 'Sexy MF' (1992) and the steamy 'Orgasm' (1994) are all hot contenders. In 1991, on the *Diamonds and Pearls* album, it was 'Gett Off' that got us bothered. Funky and filthy, 'Gett Off' entered the upper echelons of the charts in the UK and beyond, and got many of us wondering about those "23 positions in a one-night stand...".

5 THINGS U NEVER KNEW

0 PHONES

Prince didn't have a mobile phone and didn't like computers much either: "All these computers and digital gadgets are no good. They just fill your head with numbers and that can't be good for you."

3121

Prince loved number titles in his songs: '1999', 'Love 2 the 9's', '319', '3 x 2 = 6', '777-9311' and many others. The number 3121 was a particular favourite: he named his 31st album, a nightclub and a fragrance after it. In fact, 3121 was the number of the home he rented in Mulholland Drive, Beverly Hills, from NBA star Carlos Boozer.

I WOULD DIE 4 U

Prince often replaced words with numbers in song titles. 'To', 'Two' or 'Too' became '2', and 'for' became '4'. Prince used this distinctive style of writing for his autobiography, *The Beautiful Ones,* published posthumously in 2019.

40 GUITARS/ 22-PIECE BAND

Star Wars creator George Lucas and Mellody Hobson asked Prince to play at their wedding reception in 2013. It was a small event but Prince went all *Star Wars* with his guitars and backing band.

4 INCHES

Prince had 3,000 pairs of boots custom-made by cobbler to the Hollywood stars, Andre No. 1. All were made to the same specification, with heels that boosted his height by 3.33–4in. (85–100mm).

PRINCE ROGERS NELSON

03
WORK

"WHEN I'M ONSTAGE, I'M OUT OF BODY. THAT'S WHAT THE REHEARSALS, THE PRACTISING, THE PLAYING IS FOR. YOU WORK TO A PLACE WHERE YOU'RE ALL OUT OF BODY. AND THAT'S WHEN SOMETHING HAPPENS. YOU REACH A PLANE OF CREATIVITY AND INSPIRATION. A PLANE WHERE EVERY SONG THAT HAS EVER EXISTED AND EVERY SONG THAT WILL EXIST IN THE FUTURE IS RIGHT THERE IN FRONT OF YOU. AND YOU GO WITH IT FOR AS LONG AS IT TAKES."

—Prince, Essence Festival, 2014

PROLIFIC PRINCE: THE ALBUMS

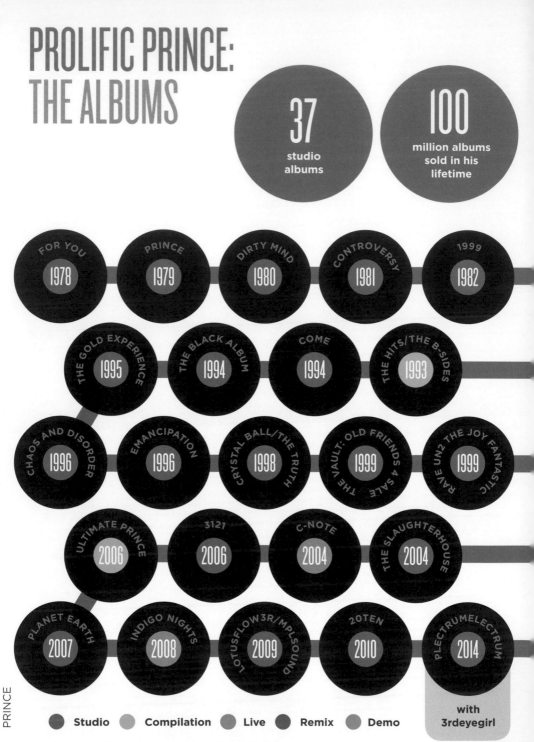

37 studio albums

100 million albums sold in his lifetime

FOR YOU 1978

PRINCE 1979

DIRTY MIND 1980

CONTROVERSY 1981

1999 1982

THE GOLD EXPERIENCE 1995

THE BLACK ALBUM 1994

COME 1994

THE HITS/THE B-SIDES 1993

CHAOS AND DISORDER 1996

EMANCIPATION 1996

CRYSTAL BALL/THE TRUTH 1998

THE VAULT: OLD FRIENDS 4 SALE 1999

RAVE UN2 THE JOY FANTASTIC 1999

ULTIMATE PRINCE 2006

3121 2006

C-NOTE 2004

THE SLAUGHTERHOUSE 2004

PLANET EARTH 2007

INDIGO NIGHTS 2008

LOTUSFLOW3R/MPLSOUND 2009

20TEN 2010

PLECTRUMELECTRUM 2014

with 3rdeyegirl

● Studio   ● Compilation   ● Live   ● Remix   ● Demo

Prince burst onto the music scene in 1978 with his sassy funk debut album *For You*. By 1984, with the worldwide success of the *Purple Rain* album, he was fast becoming a superstar with a flair for funk-soul-disco-pop dance grooves. Later albums traversed the genres, fusing jazz and rap, and on occasion stripping back to just piano and microphone. Over five decades, Prince released 37 studio LPs, but there is plenty more to come. In the Vault, at Paisley Park, there were rumoured to be thousands of unreleased demos; reports claim these have now been moved to storage elsewhere.

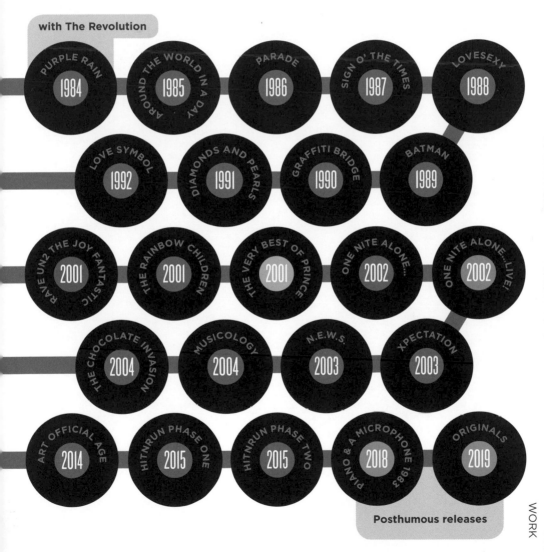

with The Revolution

PURPLE RAIN	AROUND THE WORLD IN A DAY	PARADE	SIGN O' THE TIMES	LOVESEXY
1984	1985	1986	1987	1988

LOVE SYMBOL	DIAMONDS AND PEARLS	GRAFFITI BRIDGE	BATMAN
1992	1991	1990	1989

RAVE UN2 THE JOY FANTASTIC	THE RAINBOW CHILDREN	THE VERY BEST OF PRINCE	ONE NITE ALONE...	ONE NITE ALONE...LIVE!
2001	2001	2001	2002	2002

THE CHOCOLATE INVASION	MUSICOLOGY	N.E.W.S.	XPECTATION
2004	2004	2003	2003

ART OFFICIAL AGE	HITNRUN PHASE ONE	HITNRUN PHASE TWO	PIANO & A MICROPHONE 1983	ORIGINALS
2014	2015	2015	2018	2019

Posthumous releases

Packaged in purple, a precursor of things to come, the *1999* album was composed, performed, produced and arranged by Prince. Kicking off with '1999', the tone was set for a wild dance party, but it was disco-funk, floor-filling 'Little Red Corvette' that was the album's first big hit and marked Prince's debut in the US Top 10 singles chart. Loaded with funky guitars, synths and drum-machine, this album defined the '80s sound. By the end of 1982, Prince was a household name and *Rolling Stone* had crowned him Artist of the Year.

RELEASED: 27 OCTOBER 1982

1. 1999 (6.22)
2. Little Red Corvette (4.58)
3. Delirious (3.56)

4. Let's Pretend
   We're Married (7.20)
5. D.M.S.R. (8.15)

6. Automatic (9.27)
7. Something in the Water
   (Does Not Compute) (4.00)
8. Free (5.08)

9. Lady Cab Driver (8.25)
10. All the Critics Love U
    in New York (5.55)
11. International Lover (6.37)

DOUBLE ALBUM

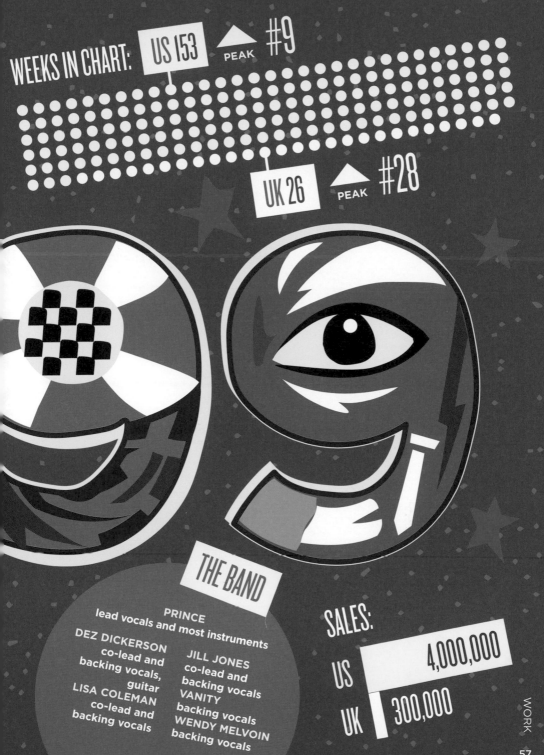

WEEKS IN CHART: US 153 ▲ PEAK #9

UK 26 ▲ PEAK #28

THE BAND

PRINCE
lead vocals and most instruments

DEZ DICKERSON
co-lead and
backing vocals,
guitar

JILL JONES
co-lead and
backing vocals

LISA COLEMAN
co-lead and
backing vocals

VANITY
backing vocals

WENDY MELVOIN
backing vocals

SALES:
US 4,000,000
UK 300,000

After the success of his fifth album, *1999*, Prince's label encouraged him to head back into the studio. Always the experimenter, Prince had other ideas, and what came next would make him a superstar. Not content with producing another album, Prince asked his management team to look into financing for a motion picture starring himself. Released in 1984, *Purple Rain* was a rock musical loosely based on Prince's life, but it was the soundtrack that made him a household name. Selling more than 1.5 million copies in its first week, the album quickly rose to number one and stayed there for 24 weeks. On 4 August 1984, the album, the film and the lead single, 'When Doves Cry', were all at number one in their respective charts.

ALBUM TRACKS

1. **LET'S GO CRAZY (4:39)**
2. **TAKE ME WITH U (3:54)**
3. **THE BEAUTIFUL ONES (5:13)**
4. **COMPUTER BLUE (3:59)**
5. **DARLING NIKKI (4:14)**
6. **WHEN DOVES CRY (5:54)**
7. **I WOULD DIE 4 U (2:49)**
8. **BABY I'M A STAR (4:24)**
9. **PURPLE RAIN (8:41)**

Purple

PRINCE – LEAD VOCALS AND ALL INSTRUMENTS
LISA COLEMAN – KEYBOARDS AND BACKING VOCALS
WENDY MELVOIN – GUITAR AND BACKING VOCALS
MATT FINK – KEYBOARDS AND VOCALS
BROWN MARK – BASS GUITAR AND VOCALS
BOBBY Z – DRUMS
NOVI NOVOG – VIOLIN, VIOLA
DAVID COLEMAN – CELLO
SUZIE KATAYAMA – CELLO
APOLLONIA – CO-LEAD VOCALS
JILL JONES – CO-LEAD AND BACKING VOCALS

FIRST WEEK US ALBUM SALES

1.5m

24 WEEKS ON
BILLBOARD
CHARTS AT

#1

WEEKS ON
BILLBOARD
CHARTS

122

Rain

WEEKS
IN UK
CHARTS

86

TOTAL
ALBUM SALES
WORLDWIDE

25m

HIGHEST
UK CHART
POSITION

#7

PARENTAL ADVISORY

Purple Rain, the album, contains a number of sexual themes. After Tipper Gore –
later Second Lady of the United States – caught her 11-year-old daughter listening
to it, she founded the Parents Music Resource Centre. This led to the mandatory use
of a warning label on albums with explicit content.

PRINCE AT THE MOVIES

Prince made his acting debut in *Purple Rain,* playing a struggling musician named 'The Kid'. Filming took place in Minneapolis at venues such as the First Avenue nightclub where he played regularly in the early days of his career. Both the film and the soundtrack were huge commercial successes, with the film winning an Oscar for Best Original Song Score and Prince earning an NAACP Image Award for Outstanding Actor in a Motion Picture. *Purple Rain* remains one of the top-selling soundtracks of all time, so how does it compare to the other greats...?

The graph below shows number of soundtrack albums sold in the US to the nearest million.

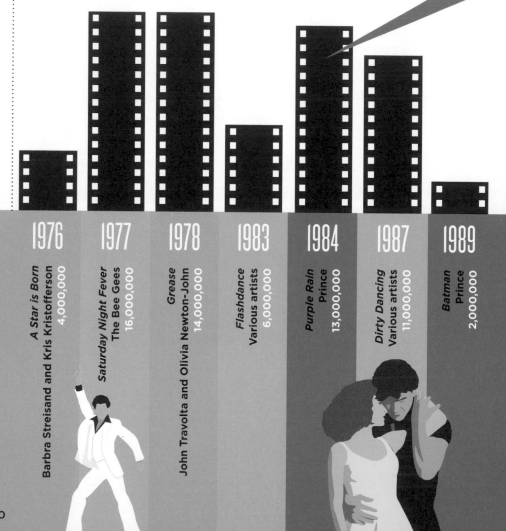

1976	1977	1978	1983	1984	1987	1989
A Star is Born Barbra Streisand and Kris Kristofferson 4,000,000	*Saturday Night Fever* The Bee Gees 16,000,000	*Grease* John Travolta and Olivia Newton-John 14,000,000	*Flashdance* Various artists 6,000,000	*Purple Rain* Prince 13,000,000	*Dirty Dancing* Various artists 11,000,000	*Batman* Prince 2,000,000

100

songs written by Prince and given to the movie's director to choose from. The song 'When Doves Cry' was not included on the original list.

Prince directed and starred in *Under the Cherry Moon* (1986), *Graffiti Bridge* (the 1990 sequel to *Purple Rain*) and the concert film *Sign o' the Times* (1987). He also wrote the soundtrack for Tim Burton's *Batman* in 1989.

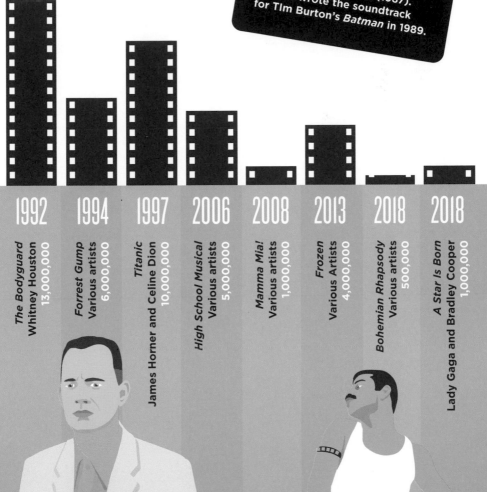

1992	1994	1997	2006	2008	2013	2018	2018
The Bodyguard Whitney Houston 13,000,000	*Forrest Gump* Various artists 6,000,000	*Titanic* James Horner and Celine Dion 10,000,000	*High School Musical* Various artists 5,000,000	*Mamma Mia!* Various artists 1,000,000	*Frozen* Various Artists 4,000,000	*Bohemian Rhapsody* Various artists 500,000	*A Star Is Born* Lady Gaga and Bradley Cooper 1,000,000

WORK

GUITAR ROYALTY

Prince was a music junkie who fed his addiction with an extensive collection of guitars and other instruments. Like many successful guitarists, he collected an array of vintage Gibson Les Pauls, and Fender Stratocasters and Telecasters (some of which he sprayed gold or covered in fake fur). But Prince was the master of iconography, and this certainly extended to his guitars. He was a brilliant rock soloist, so the sound of his instruments and amps was paramount. But you also had to have the look...

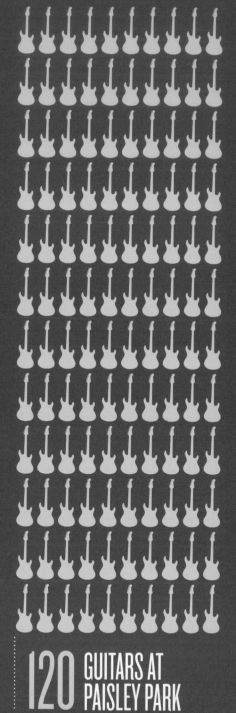

£700,000

Prince's teal-blue Cloud sold at auction in Los Angeles, 2017

£225,000

Prince's yellow Cloud sold at auction in New York, 2018

120 **GUITARS AT PAISLEY PARK**

ICONIC AXES

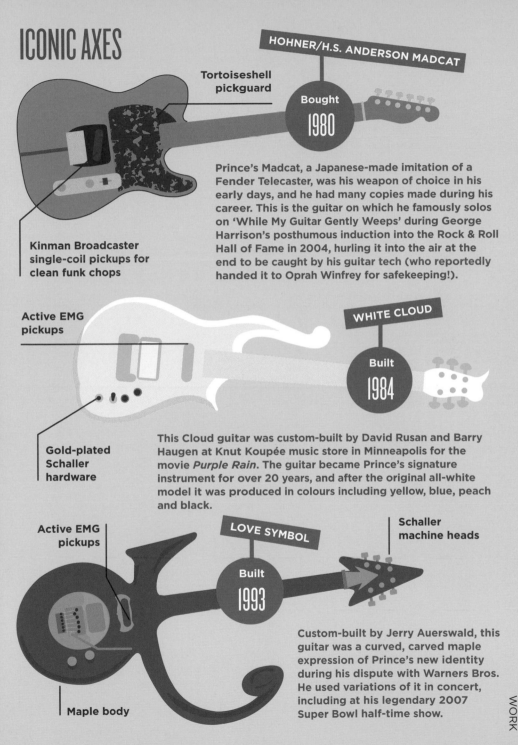

Tortoiseshell pickguard

Bought
1980

Prince's Madcat, a Japanese-made imitation of a Fender Telecaster, was his weapon of choice in his early days, and he had many copies made during his career. This is the guitar on which he famously solos on 'While My Guitar Gently Weeps' during George Harrison's posthumous induction into the Rock & Roll Hall of Fame in 2004, hurling it into the air at the end to be caught by his guitar tech (who reportedly handed it to Oprah Winfrey for safekeeping!).

Kinman Broadcaster single-coil pickups for clean funk chops

Active EMG pickups

WHITE CLOUD

Built
1984

Gold-plated Schaller hardware

This Cloud guitar was custom-built by David Rusan and Barry Haugen at Knut Koupée music store in Minneapolis for the movie *Purple Rain*. The guitar became Prince's signature instrument for over 20 years, and after the original all-white model it was produced in colours including yellow, blue, peach and black.

Active EMG pickups

LOVE SYMBOL

Schaller machine heads

Built
1993

Custom-built by Jerry Auerswald, this guitar was a curved, carved maple expression of Prince's new identity during his dispute with Warners Bros. He used variations of it in concert, including at his legendary 2007 Super Bowl half-time show.

Maple body

WORK

Purple Rain

TOUR 1984/5

Prince's fifth tour was his biggest and most theatrical to date. Ever the perfectionist, he demanded stunning sets and costumes, slick pyrotechnics and a band that could dance while playing their instruments.

98 SHOWS

32 VENUES

OVER 1.7 MILLION TICKETS SOLD

3 hour soundchecks

$500 The amount Prince docked from a band member's pay packet for missing a cue or making a mistake

First night: 4 November 1984 Joe Louis Arena, Detroit, Michigan

Last night: 7 April 1985 Orange Bowl, Miami, Florida

TOUR HIGHLIGHT

23 February 1985
The Forum, LA
5 x costume changes
30-minute version of 'Purple Rain'
Encore: Madonna and Bruce Springsteen sing 'Baby I'm a Star'

PRINCE

ONE NIGHT ONLY

4 FEBRUARY 2007

SUPER BOWL

XLI • HALFTIME SHOW

Prince's performance at Super Bowl XLI is regarded as one of the greatest Super Bowl half-time appearances. Storms lashed the stage as Prince whipped up a medley of covers culminating in an epic rendition of 'Purple Rain'.

Performance length:
11 MINUTES 50 SECONDS

STORMY WEATHER

DOLPHIN STADIUM FLORIDA

Audience:
75,000

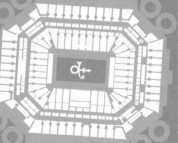

Set list:
1. We Will Rock You
2. Let's Go Crazy
3. 1999/
   Baby I'm a Star
4. Proud Mary
5. All Along the
   Watchtower/
   Best of You
6. Purple Rain

140 MILLION TV VIEWERS

$2.6 million for 30-second television commercial

INDIANAPOLIS COLTS V CHICAGO BEARS

ONE-MAN BAND

At the age of 16, Prince told Todd Rundgren: "I play everything and I'm real talented." Possibly he was looking for an 'in' with Rundgren, another multi-instrumentalist, but he wasn't exaggerating. He had been playing since the age of five, and he could play everything from piano, guitar, bass and drums to marimbas and the Mellotron. Prince once confessed to saxophonist Marcus Anderson: "I am my favourite on guitar. I'm my favourite on keys and I'm my favourite drummer too. I know what music should sound like in my head."

7 Prince's age when he learned to play the *Batman* theme on piano

120 Number of guitars in Prince's custom guitar collection

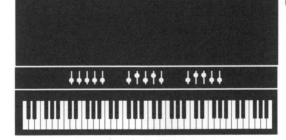

These are some of the instruments Prince could play...

01	Acoustic guitar	12	Drums
02	Bass guitar	13	Electric piano
03	Bass synth	14	Flute
04	ARP string ensemble	15	Piano
05	Bongos	16	Trumpet
06	Marimba	17	Mini Moog
07	Electric guitar	18	Slapsticks
08	Finger cymbals	19	Mellotron
09	Harmonica	20	Poly Moog
10	Congas	21	Violin
11	Clavinet		

Prince played 27 instruments on his debut album *For You*, which was released in 1978.

ALL THE COLOURS

Prince is synonymous with purple, but all the colours of the rainbow permeate his life and songs. His first wife Mayte claimed that Paisley Park was regularly redecorated a

1993	1985	2009	2012	1988
Pink Cashmere	**Raspberry Beret**	**Crimson and Clover**	**Redhead Stepchild**	**Scarlet Pussy**
1976	2012	1985	1991	1989
Amber Eyes	**Yellow Gold**	**Yellow**	**Whispering Dandelions**	**Lemon Crush**
1991	2001	2004	1996	2014
Cream	**Underneath the Cream**	**Silver Tongue**	**White Mansion**	**Whitecaps**
1993	1984	1983	1978	1989
Get Blue	**Computer Blue**	**Blue Love**	**So Blue**	**Blues In C** (If I Had a Harem)
1995	2004	2019	1984	2013
Purple Medley	**Purple House**	**Purple Music**	**Purple Rain**	**Shade of Umber**
1993	2006	2015		
Black MF in the House	**Black Sweat**	**Black Muse**		

different colour and new cars were customized in the same hue. Scarlet, crimson and red feature almost as much as his beloved purple in his lavish wardrobe and guitar collection. In August 2017, Prince's sister Tyka Nelson revealed that his favourite colour was actually orange, although the Purple One never used orange in a song title.

Red Scarlett 1993	**Little Red Corvette** 1982	**Cherry, Cherry** 1995	**Under the Cherry Moon** 1986	**Tangerine** 1999
Gold 1996	**Golden Parachute** 2001	**The Gold Standard** 2014	**Goldie's Parade** 1993	**Milk & Honey** 2006
Jadestone 1991	**Misty Blue** 2008	**Blue Light** 1992	**Love on a Blue Train** 1987	**Blue Limousine** 1984
Blues In G (I Got Some Help I Don't Need) 1984	**Indigo Nights** 2008	**Violet Blue** 1987	**Violet the Organ Grinder** 1991	**Purple and Gold** 2010
Cinnamon Girl 2004	**Cold Coffee and Cocaine** 2018	**Starfish and Coffee** 1987	**Chocolate Box** 2009	**Chocolate** 1990

In September 2017 Prince's half sister Sharon L. Nelson claimed that purple was Prince's favourite colour after all! She revealed that he "was fond of many colours in the rainbow, he especially loved the colour purple because it represented royalty" and "the color purple always made him feel Princely".

RELEASED: 30 MARCH 1987

THE BAND

PRINCE
lead vocals and
most instruments

WENDY MELVOIN
guitar and backing
vocals
SHEILA E
drums, percussion
and rap
MATT FINK
keyboards

BOBBY Z
drums
MIKO WEAVER
guitar
ERIC LEEDS
sax
JILL JONES
vocals
SHEENA EASTON
contributing artist
CLARE FISCHER
strings

BROWN MARK
bass guitar
ATLANTA BLISS
trumpet
SUSANNAH MELVOIN
backing vocals
LISA COLEMAN
backing vocals,
Fairlight sitar, wooden
flute, keyboards and
backing vocals

Prince approached
Warner Bros with
a triple album
called *Crystal Ball*.
Double-album *Sign
o' the Times* was the
compromise.

SIGN O'

At the final gig of the Parade
tour Prince smashed his *Purple
Rain* guitar, an act that heralded a
new era. Back in LA, Prince disbanded
The Revolution and retreated to Paisley
Park where he added substantially to
his basement tape vault. The mood
was reflective; a sonic comedown from
the excesses of the 1980s. AIDS, drugs,
abandoned babies, nuclear bombs and
social chaos were on the agenda. Sensual
soul, pop, rock, electro-funk, gospel and
even hip hop were channelled in a bout of
creativity that harvested at least five albums'
worth of material. Prince's ninth album, the
double-disc *Sign o' the Times*, is the final
edit; a work that was voted finest album of
the 1980s by *Rolling Stone* magazine and is
often cited as Prince's 'masterpiece'.

"*SIGN O' THE TIMES* IS THE
SOUND OF THE LATE '80S – IT'S
THE SOUND OF THE GOOD TIMES
COLLAPSING AND HOW ALL
THAT DOUBT AND FEAR CAN BE
IGNORED IF YOU JUST DANCE
THOSE PROBLEMS AWAY."

—Stephen Thomas
Erlewine, AllMusic

Robert Smith of The Cure called 'Starfish and Coffee' one of his favourite songs. Prince died on Smith's birthday and The Cure played St Paul, Minnesota, on Prince's birthday in 2016. The singer played a purple guitar decorated with the lyrics to 'Starfish and Coffee' as a tribute to his hero.

THE TIMES

One of Prince's many pseudonyms, guest vocalist 'Camille' was created by speeding up the playback on his own vocals.

DOUBLE ALBUM

1. Sign o' the Times (4.57)
2. Play in the Sunshine (5.05)
3. Housequake (4.42)
4. The Ballad of Dorothy Parker (4.01)
5. It (5.09)
6. Starfish and Coffee (2.50)
7. Slow Love (4.22)
8. Hot Thing (5.39)
9. Forever in My Life (3.30)
10. U Got the Look (3.47)
11. If I Was Your Girlfriend (5.01)
12. Strange Relationship (4.01)
13. I Could Never Take the Place of Your Man (6.29)
14. The Cross (4.48)
15. It's Gonna Be a Beautiful Night (9.01)
16. Adore (6.30)

ALBUMS SOLD

US PEAK ▲ #6   1,000,000

UK PEAK ▲ #4   300,000

COLLABORATIONS

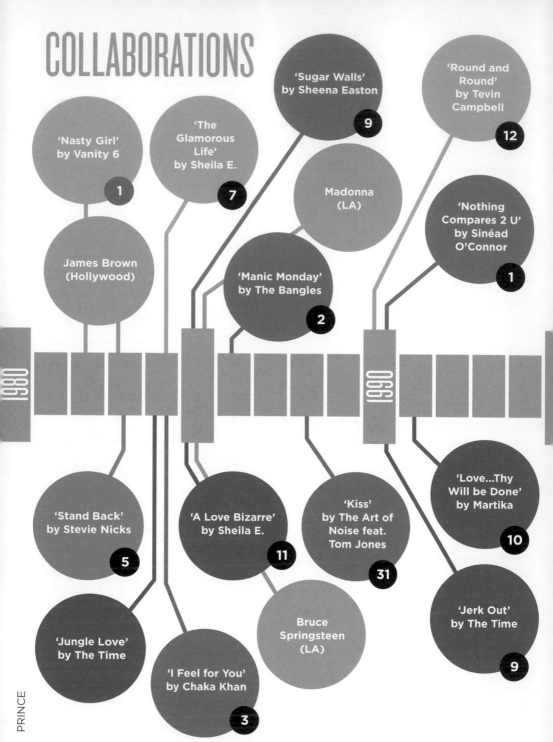

'Sugar Walls' by Sheena Easton — 9

'Round and Round' by Tevin Campbell — 12

'Nasty Girl' by Vanity 6 — 1

'The Glamorous Life' by Sheila E. — 7

Madonna (LA)

'Nothing Compares 2 U' by Sinéad O'Connor — 1

James Brown (Hollywood)

'Manic Monday' by The Bangles — 2

1980

1990

'Love...Thy Will be Done' by Martika — 10

'Stand Back' by Stevie Nicks — 5

'A Love Bizarre' by Sheila E. — 11

'Kiss' by The Art of Noise feat. Tom Jones — 31

'Jerk Out' by The Time — 9

'Jungle Love' by The Time

'I Feel for You' by Chaka Khan — 3

Bruce Springsteen (LA)

KEY

- ● Written and produced by Prince
- ● Co-written and produced by Prince
- ● Live guests
- ● US Hot Dance Club Chart
- ● Written by Prince
- ● Co-written by Prince
- ● US Hot 100 Position

ARTISTS SIGNED TO PAISLEY PARK RECORD LABEL:

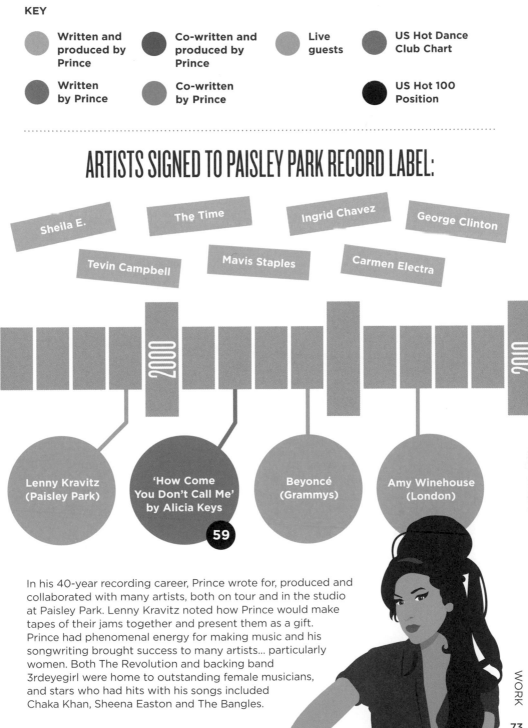

Sheila E.

The Time

Ingrid Chavez

George Clinton

Tevin Campbell

Mavis Staples

Carmen Electra

2000

2010

Lenny Kravitz (Paisley Park)

'How Come You Don't Call Me' by Alicia Keys

59

Beyoncé (Grammys)

Amy Winehouse (London)

In his 40-year recording career, Prince wrote for, produced and collaborated with many artists, both on tour and in the studio at Paisley Park. Lenny Kravitz noted how Prince would make tapes of their jams together and present them as a gift. Prince had phenomenal energy for making music and his songwriting brought success to many artists... particularly women. Both The Revolution and backing band 3rdeyegirl were home to outstanding female musicians, and stars who had hits with his songs included Chaka Khan, Sheena Easton and The Bangles.

WORK

73

ROYAL RIDERS

Like many rock stars, Prince would provide a list of backstage demands, called 'riders', before agreeing to perform. Some of these have become the stuff of legend, such as his reported request in 2007 for a luxury five-bedroom home to be built near the O2 Arena in London. He was also said to have requested a limousine to transport him 25 yards (23m) from his dressing room to a festival stage. But the list of riders for his 2012 tour suggests simply a taste for the good life.

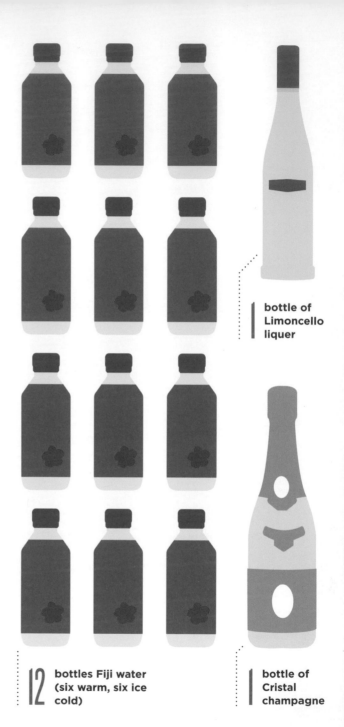

bottle of Limoncello liquer

box of Yogi Tea Mayan Cocoa Spice herbal tea

12 **bottles Fiji water (six warm, six ice cold)**

bottle of Cristal champagne

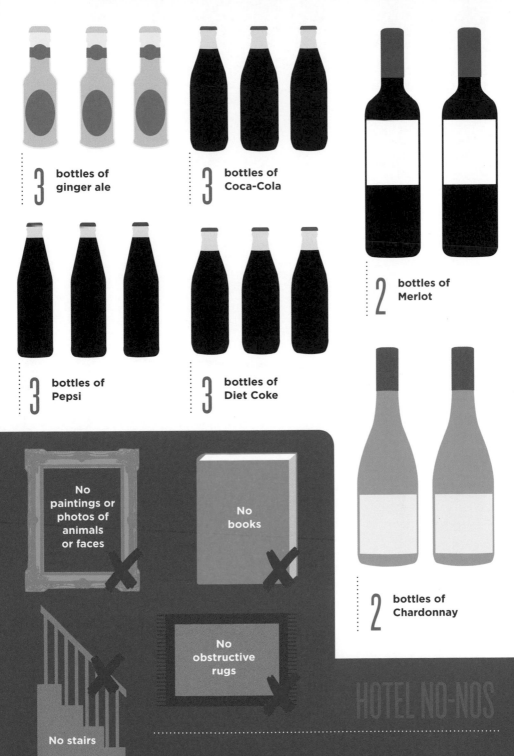

3 bottles of ginger ale

3 bottles of Coca-Cola

2 bottles of Merlot

3 bottles of Pepsi

3 bottles of Diet Coke

No paintings or photos of animals or faces

No books

No obstructive rugs

2 bottles of Chardonnay

No stairs

TOUR DE FORCE

Throughout his career, Prince maintained a demanding tour schedule. He was an electrifying live performer, combining virtuoso singing and guitar playing with exhausting dance routines. And, as if the headline performances were not gruelling enough, he was also famous for his aftershow parties. In 1985, after the success (and excess) of the Purple Rain Tour, Prince announced that he would not perform live again. In fact, he toured extensively for the rest of his life and gave a stunning solo performance in Atlanta just a week before his death.

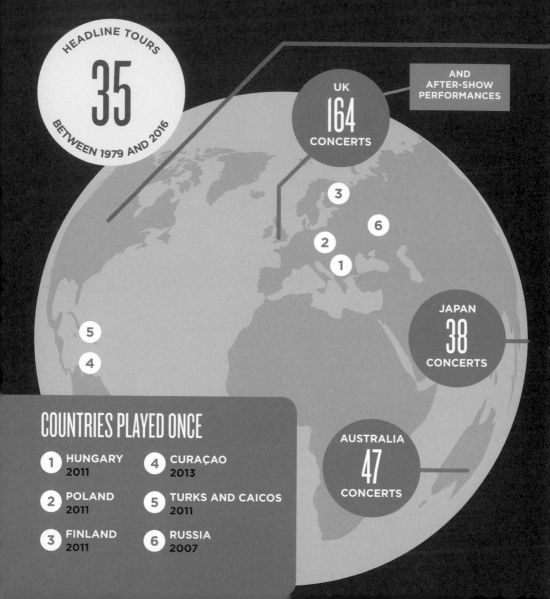

HEADLINE TOURS
35
BETWEEN 1979 AND 2016

UK
164
CONCERTS

AND AFTER-SHOW PERFORMANCES

3

6

2

1

JAPAN
38
CONCERTS

5

4

AUSTRALIA
47
CONCERTS

COUNTRIES PLAYED ONCE

1 **HUNGARY** 2011

4 **CURAÇAO** 2013

2 **POLAND** 2011

5 **TURKS AND CAICOS** 2011

3 **FINLAND** 2011

6 **RUSSIA** 2007

US CONCERTS

Bar chart of US concerts per year:

Year	Concerts
1979	5
1980	70
1981	50
1982	74
1983	60
1984	53
1985	65
1986	19
1987	7
1988	45
1989	5
1990	3
1991	12
1992	6
1993	44
1994	36
1995	34
1996	18
1997	110
1998	53
1999	32
2000	46
2001	33
2002	50
2003	6
2004	117
2005	16
2006	64
2007	72
2008	18
2009	16
2010	12
2011	47
2012	9
2013	52
2014	20
2015	23
2016	12

ADMIT ONE

FIRST TOUR
26 November 1979
17 February 1980

PRINCE TOUR

57 SHOWS

THE EARTH TOUR
1 August—21 September 2007

21 NIGHTS

O2 Arena, London
351,527 TICKETS SOLD

TICKET PRICE **£31.21**

MUSICOLOGY TOUR

$61 AVERAGE TICKET PRICE / **$87.4** MILLION GROSS PROFIT

2004

88 SHOWS

ADMIT ONE

FINAL TOUR
PIANO & A MICROPHONE TOUR
16 February
14 April 2016 | **20** | SHOWS

Australia, New Zealand, Canada, USA

PRINCE

THE SINGLES

UK No. 1
'The Most Beautiful
Girl in the World'
(1994)

16 UK Top 10
singles

40 UK Top 40
singles

5 US Billboard
chart No. 1s:
'When Doves
Cry' (1984)
'Let's Go Crazy'
(1984)
'Cream' (1991)
'Kiss' (1986)
'Batdance'
(1989)

3 singles peaked
at No. 2 on US
Billboard charts
'U Got The
Look' (1987)
'Purple Rain'
(1984)
'Raspberry
Beret' (1985)

19 US BILLBOARD CHART TOP 10s

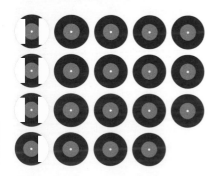

BIG SELLERS

WHEN DOVES CRY

US 2,000,000

UK 200,000

PURPLE RAIN

US 1,000,000

UK 600,000

KISS

US 1,000,000

UK 400,000

BATDANCE

US 1,000,000

UK 200,000

THE MOST BEAUTIFUL GIRL IN THE WORLD

US 500,000

UK 200,000

KEY

Platinum   Gold   Silver

PRINCE ROGERS NELSON

04
LEGACY

"FEW ARTISTS HAVE INFLUENCED THE SOUND AND TRAJECTORY OF POPULAR MUSIC MORE DISTINCTLY, OR TOUCHED QUITE SO MANY PEOPLE WITH THEIR TALENT... HE WAS A VIRTUOSO INSTRUMENTALIST, A BRILLIANT

BANDLEADER, AND AN ELECTRIFYING PERFORMER. 'A STRONG SPIRIT TRANSCENDS RULES,' PRINCE ONCE SAID — AND NOBODY'S SPIRIT WAS STRONGER, BOLDER, OR MORE CREATIVE."

—President Barack Obama, 21 April 2016

LOVE SYMBOL #2

Throughout his long career Prince was always associated with the colour purple, which infused his music, his clothing, his instruments and his pseudonyms. In 2017, Prince was honoured with his own official shade. The Pantone Color Institute, the global colour authority, worked with the Prince estate to create a standardized colour to represent and honour the singer. The chosen hue, named Love Symbol #2, was inspired by his custom-made Yamaha purple piano.

PANTONE

Pantone was originally established in New Jersey in the 1950s as a commercial printing company. Employee Lawrence Herbert used his knowledge to systematize and simplify the company's pigments and inks, and in 1962 took control and renamed them 'Pantone'. The company became known for its Pantone Matching System and Pantone Guides, which allowed designers to colour-match specific colours. The Pantone Color Institute now creates exclusive shades for iconic brands.

BATES MOTEL BLUE
(A&E Networks)

JAY-Z BLUE
(Jay-Z)

US ARMY GREEN
(US Army, 19 shades)

PIPER-HEIDSIECK RED
(Piper-Heidsieck)

BARBIE PINK
(Mattel)

GREY JASON WU
(Jason Wu)

GAP BLUE
(Gap)

MINION YELLOW
(*Despicable Me* franchise)

TIFFANY BLUE
(Tiffany & Co.)

PRINCE IN NUMBERS

130 MILLION RECORDS SOLD WORLDWIDE

2 DOVES
owned by Prince, named Majesty and Divinity, who get a singing credit on Prince's 2002 album *One Nite Alone...*

2,000 PAIRS OF SHOES
in the archive at Paisley Park

$300 MILLION
estimated value of his fortune

6 MILLION tweets in the seven hours after Prince's death

7 YEARS
in which Prince was known only as the 'Love Symbol'

$25 MILLION
earned in 2016 by Prince, the fifth highest-earning deceased celebrity

40+ SONGS
played in Prince's two-set final show at Atlanta's Fox Theatre in April 2016

35 JACKETS
and pairs of trousers from the Purple Rain Tour of 1984–5 in the Paisley Park archives

61 SECONDS

of Julia Roberts singing Prince's 'Kiss' in the bath before being rudely interrupted by Richard Gere in *Pretty Woman*

AND THE AWARD GOES TO...

7 GRAMMY AWARDS

7 BRIT AWARDS

5 AMERICAN MUSIC AWARDS

4 MTV VIDEO MUSIC AWARDS

1 ACADEMY AWARD

1 GOLDEN GLOBE

PULLING POWER

300 PEOPLE

in the crowd at the Capri Theatre, Minneapolis, in 1979

140 MILLION

television viewers of the Super Bowl XLI Halftime Show at Miami Gardens, Prince's biggest audience ever

37 STUDIO ALBUMS

106 SINGLES

2016 was the annus horribilis when it came to losing superstars. David Bowie's death on 10 January unleashed a wave of mourning rarely seen in the music world. When Prince passed away on 21 April the world had lost two giants of the music world in quick succession.

PRINCE

Studio albums
37

Singles
106

Age
57

DIED
2016

Top-selling album
PURPLE RAIN

25
million sold worldwide

Music videos
152

Real name
PRINCE ROGERS NELSON

2 WIVES

Mayte Garcia
(1996–2000)

Manuela Testolini
(2001–6)

YEARS ACTIVE
1977–2016

MINNEAPOLIS, MINNESOTA, USA
7 JUNE 1958

BORN
1958

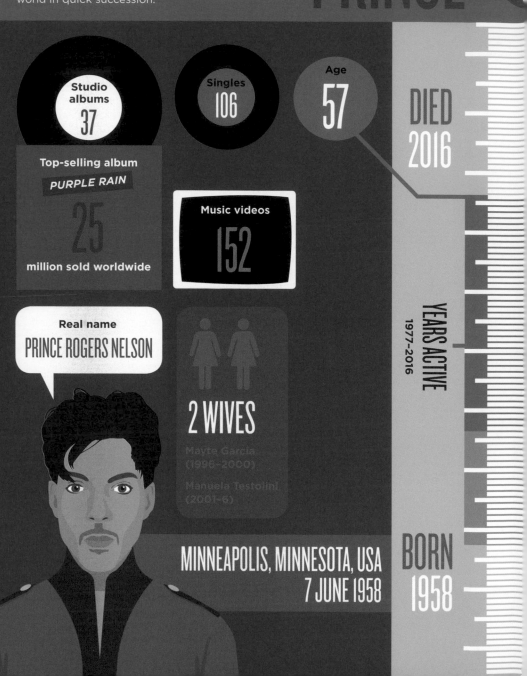

BOWIE

According to Prince he and Bowie met only once, but he did cover Bowie songs. Prince joined Nile Rodgers at the Essence Music Festival in 2014 to perform 'Let's Dance', and during his final tour he played Bowie's 'Heroes' at the piano as a tribute.

DIED
2016

YEARS ACTIVE 1964–2016

BORN
1947

Age
69

Singles
111

Studio albums
25

Top-selling album
LET'S DANCE
10.7
million sold worldwide

Music videos
51

2 WIVES
Angela Bowie
(1970–80)

Iman
(1992–2016)

Real name
DAVID ROBERT JONES

BRIXTON, LONDON, UK
8 JANUARY 1947

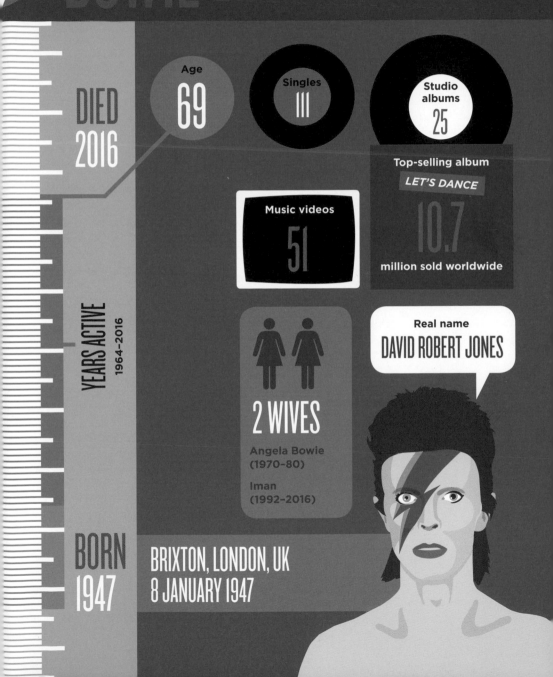

PAISLEY PARK

**7801 Audubon Rd,
Chanhassen,
Minnesota 55317, USA**

Paisley Park was the extraordinary private estate and production complex that Prince masterminded and named after his 1984 hit single. He viewed it as his private Utopia, and opted to locate it in his hometown of Minneapolis. The building looks like an industrial unit from the outside, but its interiors reveal a sensual, creative, basketball-crazed, clothing-obsessed musicaholic.

Cost to build:

$10 MILLION

Opened as a studio in

1987

Opened as a museum in

2016

VAULT

The Vault contained a treasure trove of unreleased Prince music. Only Prince knew the code and it had to be drilled open after his death. Reports claim there was enough material stored here for an album to be released every year for the next century!

ATRIUM

Prince's ashes were on display here for three years, contained inside a custom-made 3D urn, shaped like Paisley Park with his symbol on top.

When Prince was alive, two doves called Divinity and Majesty were kept in the atrium. Majesty died in 2017.

COSTUMES

Many of Prince's stage costumes are displayed throughout Paisley Park, including 'that' coat from *Purple Rain* and the aqua suit from the famous Super Bowl appearance of 2007.

4

recording studios

Total area:

65,000

sq. ft

MURALS

Paisley Park is elaborately decorated with murals of Prince and his personal heroes including Joni Mitchell, Miles Davis, Carlos Santana, Jimi Hendrix (left) and Stevie Wonder.

HOBBIES

The complex includes a ping-pong table where he once played against Michael Jackson and a basketball court where he'd shoot hoops.

BIOGRAPHIES

Lisa Coleman (b. 1960)

The keyboardist, pianist and composer was 19 when she was drafted in to play for Prince on the *Dirty Mind* album and tour. Lisa was part of famed backing band The Revolution, which scored hit albums *Purple Rain*, *Around the World in a Day* and *Parade*.

John L. Nelson (1916–2001)

Born in Louisiana, Nelson moved to Minneapolis in 1948 to become a jazz pianist. Aged five, Prince saw his father perform in his band, the Prince Rogers Trio, and was inspired to become a musician.

Matt Fink (b. 1958)

Minneapolis born and bred, keyboardist Matt Fink (aka Dr Fink) joined Prince's band in 1978 and later became a member of The Revolution. Fink mostly contributed to live performances rather than in the studio as Prince played everything on record.

Wendy Melvoin (b. 1964)

Guitarist and singer-songwriter Wendy was a childhood friend of Lisa Coleman and it was through Lisa that Wendy met Prince. In 1983, aged just 19, she joined Prince's band, The Revolution. Wendy formed the duo Wendy & Lisa in 1986.

Manuela Testolini (b. 1976)

Canadian-born lawyer and charity worker Testolini met Prince while looking for funding for a women's shelter. Prince's own charity, Love 4 One Another, helped her with the project. She eventually joined the charity and the pair married in 2001. They divorced in 2006.

Apollonia (b. 1959)

American singer, dancer and actress Apollonia Kotero was Prince's leading lady in the film *Purple Rain* as well as his lover off set. The 1984 album *Apollonia 6* was written and produced by Prince and included the future Bangles hit 'Manic Monday'.

Tyka Nelson (b. 1960)

Prince's little sister got into singing at an early age, often accompanying her brother while he played piano. A performer in her own right, Tyka released four albums between 1988 and 2008. Together with Prince's five half-siblings, she inherited his $200 million estate.

Sheila E. (b. 1957)

Often called the 'Queen of Percussion', Sheila Escovedo and Prince had a brief romance and professional dalliance in the 1980s when she supported him on the Purple Rain Tour. They recorded hundreds of songs together.

Morris Hayes (b. 1962)

Musical director and keyboard player Morris played with Prince from 1992 to 2012, making him his longest-serving musical companion. Morris was playing with the Time when Prince spotted his talent and asked him to join his Diamonds and Pearls Tour.

Carmen Electra (b. 1972)

The dancer and model moved to Minneapolis in 1991 and soon became part of Prince's entourage. Prince signed Carmen to his record label, but when her solo album (produced and written by Prince) failed to take off she pursued a career in modelling and film.

Mayte Garcia (b. 1973)

Prince was so impressed by a video of Mayte dancing that he asked to meet her. 'The Most Beautiful Girl in the World' was written for her, and the couple married in 1996. Later that year, their six-day-old son died from a genetic disorder. They divorced in 2000.

Bobby Z (b. 1956)

Robert B. Rivkin (aka Bobby Z) was making music with Prince in Minneapolis in the 1970s, long before Prince was famous. Bobby played drums with Prince from 1978 to 1986, when Prince first went on tour and later as part of The Revolution.

family   band member

INDEX